Pebble®

Great African-Americans

George Washington
CARVER

by Luke Colins   Consulting Editor: Gail Saunders-Smith, PhD

CAPSTONE PRESS
a capstone imprint

Pebble Books are published by Capstone Press,
1710 Roe Crest Drive, North Mankato, Minnesota 56003
www.capstonepub.com

Library of Congress Cataloging-in-Publication Data
Colins, Luke.
George Washington Carver / by Luke Colins.
pages cm. – (Pebble Books. Great African-Americans)
Includes bibliographical references and index.
Summary: "Simple text and photographs present the life of George Washington Carver"—
Provided by publisher.
ISBN 978-1-4765-3957-7 (library binding)
ISBN 978-1-4765-5161-6 (paperback)
ISBN 978-1-4765-6018-2 (ebook PDF)
1. Carver, George Washington, 1864?–1943—Juvenile literature. 2. African American
agriculturists—Biography—Juvenile literature. 3. Agriculturists—United States—Biography—
Juvenile literature. I. Title.
S417.C3C655 2014
630.92—dc23
[B]   2013024397

Editorial Credits
Ashlee Suker, designer; Wanda Winch, media researcher; Laura Manthe, production specialist

Photo Credits
Corbis, cover, 16, Bettmann, 18; Library of Congress: Prints and Photographs Division/Arthur
Rothstein, 20, Frances Benjamin Johnson, 10, 12; Shutterstock: Izf, leaf design; Tuskegee
University Archives, 4, 6, 8, 14

Note to Parents and Teachers

The Great African-Americans set supports national curriculum standards for
social studies related to people, places, and environments. This book describes
and illustrates George Washington Carver. The images support early readers in
understanding the text. The repetition of words and phrases helps early readers
learn new words. This book also introduces early readers to subject-specific
vocabulary words, which are defined in the Glossary section. Early readers may
need assistance to read some words and to use the Table of Contents, Glossary,
Read More, Internet Sites, and Index sections of the book.

Printed in the United States of America in North Mankato, Minnesota.
092013   007764CGS14

Table of Contents

Meet George

George Washington Carver

was a famous scientist and teacher.

George invented more than

400 products made with peanuts

and sweet potatoes.

George in about 1876

1864 born

1875 leaves the farm

Young George

George was born in 1864 on a farm

in Missouri. He was born a slave.

George liked to study and grow plants.

By 1875 he was free to leave the farm

to go to school.

1864	1875	1884	1896
born	leaves the farm	finishes high school	finishes college

George finished high school in 1884.

He went to college in Iowa.

He studied art, plants, and farming.

George finished college in 1896.

George (center) with some of his students

1864	1875	1884	1896
born	leaves the farm	finishes high school	finishes college; begins teaching

As an Adult

George began to teach

at Tuskegee Institute in Alabama.

This school was for African-Americans.

George taught students about plants

and farming.

1864	1875	1884	1896
born	leaves the farm	finishes high school	finishes college; begins teaching

In the late 1800s farmers

in the south began

having problems growing

cotton. The soil had lost

too many nutrients.

George worked with farmers

to make the soil healthy again.

EXPERIMENT STATION
TUSKEGEE NORMAL AND INDUSTRIAL INSTITUTE.

George (front left) working with farmers

1864
born

1875
leaves
the farm

1884
finishes
high school

1896
finishes college;
begins teaching

George taught farmers

to grow other crops.

Farmers started growing peanuts

and sweet potatoes. These crops

returned nutrients to the soil.

1864	1875	1884	1896
born	leaves the farm	finishes high school	finishes college; begins teaching

Later Years

George invented many new uses

for peanuts and sweet potatoes.

He made ink and soap

from peanuts. He made

molasses, rubber, and glue

from sweet potatoes.

1896-1920
works with
farmers

1921
becomes famous for
peanut research

George shaking hands with President Roosevelt

1864	1875	1884	1896
born	leaves the farm	finishes high school	finishes college; begins teaching

George gave speeches
throughout the United States.
He told people about the uses
for peanuts. He also spoke
to Congress about
helping farmers.

1896-1920
works with
farmers

1921
becomes famous for
peanut research;
speaks to Congress

1864	1875	1884	1896
born	leaves the farm	finishes high school	finishes college; begins teaching

George died in 1943.

He is famous for inventing

new ways to use crops.

People remember him

for helping farmers.

1896-1920	1921	1943
works with farmers	becomes famous for peanut research; speaks to Congress	dies

21

Glossary

Congress—the group of people who make the laws for the United States

cotton—a plant that makes fluffy, white fibers; cotton can be used to make cloth

invent—to think up and make something new

molasses—a thick, sweet syrup

nutrient—a substance needed by a living thing to stay healthy

rubber—a strong, elastic substance used to make items such as tires, balls, and boots

slave—a person who is owned by another person; slaves are not free to choose their homes or jobs

Read More

Bennett, Doraine. *George Washington Carver.* American Heroes. Hamilton, Ga.: State Standards Publishing, 2012.

Marzollo, Jean. *The Little Plant Doctor: A Story About George Washington Carver.* New York: Holiday House, 2011.

McKissack, Patricia and Fredrick. *George Washington Carver: Scientist and Inventor.* Berkeley Heights, N.J.: Enslow Elementary, 2013.

Internet Sites

FactHound offers a safe, fun way to find Internet sites related to this book. All of the sites on FactHound have been researched by our staff.

Here's all you do:
Visit *www.facthound.com*
Type in this code: 9781476539577

Check out projects, games and lots more at
www.capstonekids.com

Critical Thinking Using the Common Core

1. The author says George was born a slave. What was life like for slaves in the United States? Use online and print resources to support your answer. (Key Ideas and Details)

2. George invented new uses for peanuts and sweet potatoes. What are some of the things you use today as a result of these new uses? (Integration of Knowledge and Ideas)

Index

Word Count: 220
Grade: 1
Early-Intervention Level: 19